What Our Readers Have Said...

Applicability

"These books are great tools that should be used as guidelines for our everyday supervisory practices. You need to take the time to do a short self-evaluation when reading them."

•

"The Pinpoint Training Series delivers information that could be used in a lot different areas."

•

"The things and problems we deal with everyday are discussed in these books."

Convenience

"I like this because I can take them with me to read at a convenient time. I feel the little time I have to spend in the office is best use on activities that directly relate to revenue opportunities. I like the short amount of time it takes to keep up with these."

•

"I prefer the self-study approach; it fits in with my schedule."

•

"I like the fact that the format allows the books to be reviewed as time permits. All work has been conducted on personal, evening/weekend time."

•

"Easy to use... if you put the time into it."

Challenge

"My thought is that the real value of these books comes into effect when doing the action plans."

•

"I like the fact that the format allows assignments to be reviewed as time permits."

Clarity

"Short and sweet. These books are easy to comprehend."

•

"Easy to use, understand, and reference if needed."

Relevance

"I have enjoyed reading these books. They are relevant to today's work environment and the ongoing change in the way we manage our workforce."

•

"I believe the contents of the Pinpoint series are excellent. It causes one to reflect on the daily dynamics in working with oneself as well as with management and peers."

Building Strong Teams

Pinpoint Leadership Skill Development Training Series

TIMOTHY F. BEDNARZ

MAJORIUM
BUSINESS PRESS

Pinpoint Leadership Skill Development Training Series
"Building Strong Teams"
Timothy F. Bednarz

Graphic design: Monika Pawlak

Majorium Business Press
2025 Main Street
Stevens Point, WI 54481
715.342.1018 • 800.654.4935

ISBN 978-1-882181-80-3

Printed in the United States of America

Introduction

The Pinpoint Leadership Skill Development Training Series is designed for targeted training and education regarding increased improvement in a specific skill or competency.

Each book within this series is designed to be easy to use, understand and apply to your job. It can be used as a basis for training individuals, as a discussion guide or as a personal training tool.

Each chapter within this book discusses a specific concept. When you have completed all eight chapters you should have a 360° perspective of the topic.

Additionally, each chapter is divided into specific sections:

- The first section provides you with an overview of the topic
- The Implications section discusses why the concept is important, and why it is important to learn and apply.
- The Strategies, Tips & Techniques to Apply section teaches how to use and apply the particular concept to your work.
- The Points to Ponder section gives you something to think about or to be discussed with a group setting. These are questions not meant to be immediately answered, but to be pondered over time.
- The Training Activity section provides you with the tools to transfer what you have learned to your job. It is designed to help create an action plan to effectively apply the concept.

Each of the topics in this series is time-tested and proven in the marketplace. They have been used by thousands of employees as training tools. Many of the users have commented that what made these books valuable, was the ability to refer to them when a problem surfaced. They indicated that they remembered reading about the exact problem. They referred back to these books and found an appropriate solution.

You will find them equally valuable as a resource in your professional development library.

Table of Contents

LEARNING OBJECTIVES:

- To identify the elements and factors of constituting a team's strength.
- To identify the critical factors and benefits of a team's strength and the impact it has.
- To understand the implications and ramifications that either enhance or diminish a team's strength.
- How to apply effective strategies to enhance team strength.
- To identify the expected results and outcomes of a team's effective use of its combined strengths.

1

Greater Power Comes from Using Multiple Strengths

A team is defined as a small number of individuals with complementary skills who are committed to a common purpose, approach and set of performance goals to which all are held mutually accountable. A more detailed examination of this definition will further elucidate strengths of the team approach.

IMPLICATIONS – WHAT THIS MEANS TO YOU

The fact that individual member efforts and overall group performance are inextricably linked makes the team the most productive performance unit an organization has at its disposal. The team is collectively responsible for specific results and will achieve them provided the performance ethic of the company is strong enough.

Within teams, each specific member's commitment to the common purpose in a set of related performance goals is of paramount importance. Each individual must believe the team's overall objective has a direct bearing on the success of the company and must collectively keep each other honest in assessing the results relative to that purpose.

This is important for leaders to consider because it is the personal commitment of individual members combined with specific team goals and a personal sense of accountability that creates an internal team's discipline, which is required for its successful development and functioning. Without internal discipline, potential team accomplishments will never be realized.

STRATEGIES, TIPS & TECHNIQUES TO APPLY

There are a number of elements that give teams their internal strength. These include:

Size

Research has shown that most teams range from 2 to 25 individuals; however, the majority number less than 10 members. Smaller teams tend to be more effective, as larger numbers of people have trouble interacting constructively as a group. Large teams are also less likely to reach timely agreements on the actionable steps required to move the team forward. Often large groups defined as teams tend to break themselves down into smaller sub-teams that are responsible for more secondary aspects of the project or problem.

Complementary Skills

In order to be effective, teams must be comprised of individuals who have the right mix of skills in three areas.

> *Technical or Functional Expertise* – Team members should possess the appropriate technical or functional know-how required for the team to accomplish its goals or objectives. Specific expertise is defined by the breadth and scope of the problem and the capabilities required to resolve it.
>
> *Problem Solving and Decision Making Skills* – Teams must be able to identify any problems and opportunities that arise. They must be able to evaluate available options and make necessary trade-offs and decisions before proceeding. Therefore, it is important for the majority of if not all team members to possess advanced problem solving and decision making skills that will allow them to effectively move the team forward.

Interpersonal Skills – Teams depend on effective communication and constructive conflict resolution. These abilities depend on the interpersonal skills and emotional intelligence of individual members, including respect, active listening and empathy as well as the ability to handle criticism, remain objective, take risks and build trust.

As leaders appoint members to their team, common sense should guide them in selecting individuals with the necessary complement of skills to achieve the team's purpose. While many teams are assembled based on more subjective personal criteria or according to a formal position description, these interpersonal areas should be considered first and foremost when selecting team members.

Common Purpose

Teams develop direction, momentum and commitment by working to shape a meaningful purpose. Effective teams invest extensive time and effort in exploring, defining and agreeing to a purpose that belongs to them both collectively and individually. Once achieved, this gives teams an identity that reaches beyond the sum total of the individuals involved. This identity keeps conflict—something both necessary and threatening to teams—constructive by providing a meaningful standard against which to resolve clashes between individual and team interests.

Common Approach

As teams require a common approach, or how they will work together to accomplish their purpose, individual members must agree on who will do specific jobs, how schedules will be set and adhered to, what skills need developing, how continuing membership is to be earned and how the group will make and modify decisions, including when and how to change it's approach to getting the job done. The agreement on operational specifics and how they integrate individual skills and advance the team's performance lies at the heart of shaping a common team approach.

Mutual Accountability

A team is not viable until it can hold itself accountable. Teams enjoying a common purpose and approach inevitably hold themselves individually and collectively more responsible for the team's performance. Teams further develop specific performance goals to provide clear yardsticks for accountability.

Accountability provides a measure of the team's quality of purpose and approach. Groups lacking mutual accountability for performance have not shaped a common purpose and approach that can sustain them as a team.

POINTS TO PONDER — SOMETHING TO THINK ABOUT

1. Does your team have a broad organizational rationale or is it defined by one individual purpose?
2. Is your team approach clear, concrete, readily understood and agreed to by all members?

TRAINING ACTIVITY — APPLICATION & ACTION PLAN

1. Examine the structure of the team that you are currently involved with by examining the following factors:
    - Size
    - Complimentary Skills
    - Common Purpose
    - Common Approach
    - Mutual Accountability
2. Using these factors, clearly define and identify the strengths and weaknesses of the team.

3. Analyze these factors and pinpoint any gaps or weaknesses within the team structure.
4. Determine how to strengthen the team's structure in order to improve its productivity.

2

How the Stages of Team Development Build Strength

Team strength is derived from the chemistry between individual members and developed over time as they learn to adapt and work together and as group synergy intensifies. This is an evolutionary process that all teams go through.

IMPLICATIONS — WHAT THIS MEANS TO YOU

The gathering of individuals together in a group does not automatically make a team. It typically takes time for groups to coalesce and form into working groups and then teams. This is an evolutionary step-by-step process that all teams go through as individual members become familiar with each other, learn to respect one another, develop boundaries and norms and, ultimately, learn to function as a team.

Team strength typically evolves through maturity and evolution: the longer teams work together, the more effective and productive they tend to become. This is due to the fact that roles and responsibilities are clarified, individuals learn the capacity and capability of other team members, and all learn to respect one another and work together toward common goals and objectives.

STRATEGIES, TIPS & TECHNIQUES TO APPLY

Teams evolve, develop and build their strengths by typically going through five individual stages. These are:

Examination

The initial gathering together of a team is normally characterized by confusion over specific roles, tasks, assignments and leadership. Due to this confusion, individual members become anxious, hostile and often overly dependent upon the team leader. Individual team members struggle with developing a group identity during this initial stage, as interactions tend to reflect relationships, alliances, biases, perceptions and antagonisms brought in from the outside.

Definition

As a result of the multiple personal agendas brought into the environment, certain predictable interactions will tend to emerge within a new team, including various levels of conflict. Struggles will arise over influence and leadership, power, tasks, roles and assignments as well as over the pace, approach and management of the team and tasks assigned to it.

Individual team members will identify the roles they wish to assume in achieving the objectives of the team. As these roles begin to crystallize, the assemblage of individuals is not yet a group, but rather a collection of individuals with a common purpose.

Identification

As team members begin to work together, personal fragmentation fades and individuals begin to identify with the group. The group starts to develop into a team as it begins to take on a unique personality created by the synergy of its members. Because individual team members find that their roles are designed to serve the overall purpose of the team, personal objectives and agendas become subordinated to the common goals of the team.

Process

During the fourth stage of development, teams learn to work effectively together. They have established the norms, goals, boundaries, roles and responsibilities that define them as a team. This is where team strength and unity is built. In addition to learning to work together as a single unit, they also learn to evaluate their effectiveness in reaching goals and objectives. They also begin to experiment with the team leadership in order to increase its overall effectiveness and productivity. This stage is where teams have matured and developed into effective working units.

Evolution

In specific circumstances, teams are created to achieve a specific goal and objective for an organization. Once the goal has been met, these teams are often dissolved. Individual members can experience a certain amount of distress once the team structure has been eliminated.

In other situations, teams continue. However, individual team members leave and join, resulting in a change in the personal dynamics of the team. This can change the synergy and personality of the team as both membership and tasks change and evolve.

POINTS TO PONDER – SOMETHING TO THINK ABOUT

1. Were you aware of how teams evolve and build strength during their development?
2. What are the biggest obstacles you see in building group strength as new teams evolve and emerge?

TRAINING ACTIVITY – APPLICATION & ACTION PLAN

1. Identify a team situation that you have participated in and analyze it using the following criteria:
    - Examination
    - Definition
    - Identification
    - Process
    - Evolution
2. Recall your experiences within this team environment and identify what specifically occurred during each stage of its development.
3. Observe the trends in the evolution of team development and strength over these five stages.

3

Team Building Roles

Team strength is built and supported by the structure, roles and responsibilities by which it is defined. These provide the mechanisms to control and channel conflict, which keep individual team members focused on achieving their specific goals and objectives.

IMPLICATIONS – WHAT THIS MEANS TO YOU

Specific team building roles contribute to both the achievement of collective goals and improvement in the overall team process. In some cases, specific team building functions are assigned to particular members, while other roles are assigned to all participants.

As a team matures and develops, leaders are empowering its individual members by fostering an environment that allows them to self-manage their particular team functions. While direct leadership involvement may recede, overall leadership effectiveness is actually enhanced by the development and facilitation of a strong team structure.

STRATEGIES, TIPS & TECHNIQUES TO APPLY

The most common organizational team building roles include the following:

Supporting

All team members assume a supporting role in which they reinforce others' points of view whether they agree or disagree with them. In actuality, supporting is the ability of team members to respect and accept the feedback and input of other team members, resulting in better contributions from all participants. Individual members realize their comments are accepted, analyzed and considered by all other members within the team as part of its responsibility, structure and process. Since comments are not discounted or minimized, each individual member is actively encouraged to provide his or her input.

Gatekeeping

Though normally assumed by the team facilitator, the gatekeeper role can be assigned to any team member. The gatekeeper ensures individual members do not monopolize discussions, and that all others have their viewpoints and perspectives solicited and acknowledged. This ensures the interaction of the entire team and prevents individual participants from being intimidated into silence.

Confronting

All team members assume the confronting role. When individual team participants behave in a manner that is detrimental to the success of the team, the others constructively confront this specific behavior. Confronting is confined to individual specific behavior, avoiding personal attacks that are highly disruptive to the team environment. Confronting behavior should be specific, narrow and defined to the particular destructive behavior exhibited within the team environment.

Mediating

The mediator role is normally assigned to either the team leader or team facilitator, whose main function is to prevent intense or prolonged disputes from erupting within the team environment. When such disputes and debates take place, individual team members typically refuse to listen or respond to one another and become polarized to one viewpoint. In these circumstances it is up to the mediator to illuminate and clarify both differences and areas of agreement. He or she also works to maintain a positive group environment by breaking down any stalls in progress and moving the entire team discussion and process forward.

Harmonizing

The harmonizing role is normally assigned to the team facilitator. However, individual team members can also assume this role, which comes into play when serious disagreements and disputes occur within the team environment. As individual members can often fail to recognize points of agreement and relationship between different positions, the harmonizer interjects summaries of the various viewpoints and points out how closely aligned they are. This helps the team build upon areas of agreement and moves the entire team process forward.

Process Observing

The team leader normally assigns the process observer role. This team member focuses his or her attention on how the team is functioning to make certain that its processes and rules are being adhered to and that a harmony of interrelationships exists.

Encompassing the dynamics of the group, the team process relates to how individual members interact with one another. The process observer pays close attention to specific interactions, notes points of conflict and disruption, and focuses his or her comments on how to build constructive behavior within the team.

Process observing is an area often minimized within the team environment, yet the very word "team" implies that collective goals are essential and that the techniques, organization, and methodology employed are vital to overall success. As most members fail to understand the impact of team dynamics and how their interaction can affect progress, the process observer role becomes essential.

Summarizing

The summarizing role is often assigned to the team facilitator, but he or she can delegate it to another individual team member. Often a team becomes overwhelmed by the intensity and depth of discussions and participants easily become confused as to the present status or point of progress. The individual assuming this role specifically summarizes the current discussion, thereby allowing the team time to gather its thoughts, clear up any confusion and restore confidence as to collective progress. The summarizing role also provides specific concrete points for the team to build upon in regard to its future progress.

POINTS TO PONDER – SOMETHING TO THINK ABOUT

1. Were you aware of the specific roles all teams must assume?
2. Do you understand how specific team building roles provide structure and guidance for all teams?

TRAINING ACTIVITY – APPLICATION & ACTION PLAN

1. On a sheet of paper list the following roles:
    - Supporting
    - Confronting
    - Gate Keeping
    - Mediating
    - Harmonizing
    - Summarizing
    - Process Observing

2. Cite specific team environment examples of how these roles are applied.
3. Determine the success or failure of these roles in each example.
4. Identify specific lessons that can be derived from each example cited.
5. Determine how to apply these lessons in future team interactions.

4

Pitfalls to Avoid While Building Team Strength

The maintenance of team strength requires ongoing leadership diligence and interaction. If leaders fail to pay attention to what is happening within the team culture and environment, it is easy to stumble into several pitfalls. Many major problems can be avoided by structured attentiveness.

IMPLICATIONS – WHAT THIS MEANS TO YOU

It is easy for leaders to begin surrendering their personal authority as they actively work to empower team members. Many assume that individual teams are automatically able to meet the responsibilities assigned to them – thus making their jobs and workloads much lighter. When this belief takes hold, it is easy for leaders to assume that their responsibilities are being effectively handled. Because of it, they generally tend to miss the undercurrents and interactions that work to undermine team strength and productivity.

Because leaders understand that empowerment is not synonymous with surrender, they play an active, ongoing role in guiding and directing the actions of their individual teams. The roles and responsibilities of individual leaders are not subjugated to their teams. Rather, teams become a mechanism for leaders to be more effective within their organization and more productive in what they need to achieve within shorter periods of time.

STRATEGIES, TIPS & TECHNIQUES TO APPLY

There are a number of common pitfalls leaders can stumble into as they develop and build their teams.

Lack of Solid Team Structure

Leaders must ensure that their teams have a solid structure in place. This includes all team members having a clear and concise understanding of their roles and responsibilities. It also includes development of and adherence to the norms, rules and boundaries established during the team's formation. Once a particular team has been established, a primary leadership responsibility is to make sure that the team adheres to its overall structure.

Not Being Observant

Within the team structure, leaders need to take a hands-off stance in regard to team matters and discussions in order to actively and impartially observe what is occurring. This enables them to be vigilant concerning internal team conflict, dominant personalities and other issues that can impact an individual team's productivity, strength and performance. Leaders cannot assume that effective team management occurs automatically within the team growth and development process. Specific attention needs to be paid to all details when any negative occurrences take place.

Allowing or Minimizing Disruptive Team Behaviors

Leaders must understand that the team culture has a specific structure that guides and directs its progress and functioning. Specific roles must be assigned to maintain this structure for an adherence to the rules, boundaries and regulations that a particular team collectively develops.

One common pitfall many leaders stumble into involves allowing individual disruptive behaviors to continue to the point where they actively hamper the team's progress. The acceptance of disruptive behaviors by leaders and other members can undermine overall team strength, as they have a tendency to intimidate less assertive participants into silence. Leaders must be vigilant for specific behaviors that inhibit the free-flow of ideas, thoughts and feedback within the team culture.

A Failure to Intervene

One of the team leader's major responsibilities is to intervene whenever required to eliminate disruptive behaviors or any other barriers that negatively impact the entire team process. When they tend to overlook specific performance-inhibiting behaviors, they are ultimately undermining team strength. It is up to team leaders to take increasingly stern measures when intervening within the team environment. These measures often start with intervention in the group setting itself; if this proves ineffective, personal intervention with the offending member(s) must be undertaken.

Displaying Bias or Favoritism

It is easy for leaders familiar with the capabilities of individual team members to display favoritism toward one member over another. However, any open display of bias will automatically cause other team members to be less open in expressing their concerns, feedback and input. Biases and favoritism have the tendency to create a situation where specific team members become dominant, which, because of their power and influence, can result in the assertion of personal agendas and overall conflict.

Not Allowing Teams to Adequately Develop and Police Themselves

It is easy for leaders, especially within a new team environment, to assume total control over the team process. They feel that it is faster and more productive to "tell and instruct" the team in what to do than allow it to develop and chart its own course.

A team learns best when it grows through its mistakes and through problems it must solve on its own. It needs to be given the room to brainstorm and create solutions, while having the freedom to police itself when internal problems and conflicts surface due to disruptive behaviors or dominant personalities.

Team strength is developed when members are allowed to work collectively through specific challenging situations and arrive at effective solutions as a result of them.

POINTS TO PONDER — SOMETHING TO THINK ABOUT

1. Can you identify any additional pitfalls you have personally observed when various team leaders attempted to build and develop team strength?
2. Would you personally tend to automatically surrender your responsibilities when developing a team, assuming that it would be able to fulfill much of your work?

TRAINING ACTIVITY — APPLICATION & ACTION PLAN

Recalling specific problems that you personally encountered while working with teams, answer the following questions.

1. Determine what you attributed these problems to.
2. What specific leadership pitfalls would you attribute to these problems?
3. What specific actions would have prevented these problems from occurring?

5

Roles That Subvert Team Strength and Performance

While some roles build team strength and performance, leaders should also understand that other roles are assumed that subvert and undermine overall team strength. These destructive behaviors not only produce a negative team environment, but can also produce a negative work environment that leaders should be aware of.

IMPLICATIONS – WHAT THIS MEANS TO YOU

In a perfect world, all individuals are always motivated to work together toward common goals and interests. In the real world, some people benefit from poor performance – their goals directly opposed to the purposes and objectives of the team. In order to assert their own personal agenda and retain power, many will work specifically against the interests of the team.

It is important for leaders to acknowledge the existence of subversive goals, roles and individuals within the organizational environment, and to intervene when teams and team members do not possess the strength to monitor and police individual behaviors. In other instances, leaders might need to intervene when disruptive individuals refuse to acknowledge the authority and power of a team over their behavior. These individuals need to have their behaviors corrected and, if they fail to respond, they need to be eliminated from the entire organizational environment.

STRATEGIES, TIPS & TECHNIQUES TO APPLY

Leaders should be familiar with the specific roles that individual team members can assume that will ultimately subvert team strength and overall performance.

Cutting or Shutting Off Discussion

Individuals that assume this role minimize individual contributions or ignore them altogether. They utilize various methods toward that end, including not allowing the individual team member to provide his or her feedback by interrupting or remaining completely silent when they do. Another common technique is to change the topic or the direction of the conversation.

Whatever the method, the purpose of cutting or shutting off discussions is to undermine the individual member's contributions to the team and, ultimately, make them feel useless. This results in anger, resentment, arguments, withdrawal of the team member being minimized, and a creation of personal barriers. Team leaders must carefully monitor for this damaging behavior, take offending parties to task, and if they cannot be brought around, remove them from the team environment.

Analyzing and Labeling

Team members that analyze and label will object to the contributions of individual team members by pigeonholing them in a way they believe describes their attitudes and motives. This immediately threatens any forward progress and can ultimately destroy the cohesiveness of the group. Rather than focus on the business at hand, these individuals sidetrack any and all discussion as the individual that has been attacked argues whether how they have been categorized is justified. Labeling is a popular technique with individuals who have nothing of substance to contribute.

Dominating

Dominant team members take over all discussion under the rationale that they alone have something to contribute and that all others have nothing of value to offer. These individuals want to sway the group through their heavy-handed behavior. They are less interested in the overall group's goals and interests and are completely focused upon their own agendas. When individual team members are allowed to dominate a team environment, it cuts overall participation and reduces the value of the team as a resource for achieving goals.

'Yes Butting'

Individual team members who assume the "Yes but" role within the team environment say one thing and mean another. Rather than directly stating their point of view or how they feel, they use the "Yes but" technique to soften the blow of disagreement.

Communicating mixed, ambiguous messages in its worst form displays hypocrisy and personal discounting of individual contributions. Leaders should understand that discussions are most effective when interaction is based on clear and unambiguous communication.

Nay Saying

Naysayers disagree with virtually everything said, and, when people tire of their contrariness, attempt to mask their negativity and underlying bitterness by claiming, "I'm just playing devil's advocate." This allows them to continue in their cynical behavior and ongoing campaign to get the team to see the futility of their efforts.

Naysayers ensure that what is right about the team's work gets completely buried. Thus, leaders must pay particular attention to this behavior when team decisions are considered to be unpleasant or risky, as members can be swayed to the naysayer's position and stymie progress.

The Leader's Responsibility
When Observing Subverting Roles and Behaviors

The presence of any of the preceding subverting behaviors requires swift and immediate intervention on the part of the team leader. If allowed to continue, these behaviors will quickly get out of hand and destroy the team's strengths, effectiveness and overall cohesiveness.

Immediate intervention can include countering statements to reverse what is being said within the group or decisive action to halt the destructive behavior and promptly rein in the offending team member. Leaders will also find that when they observe these behaviors and intervene, an open discussion of what has transpired will help minimize such behaviors in the future. Open discussion and spotlighting of these difficulties builds the team's ability to police themselves and deal with such behaviors in the future.

In cases where destructive behaviors continue, leaders may need to personally meet with the offending members outside of the group to discuss the impact of their problem and a corrective course of action. If the obstructive behaviors continue, leaders might need to take actions to eliminate these individuals from the team environment and perhaps, ultimately, from the organization.

POINTS TO PONDER — SOMETHING TO THINK ABOUT

1. When you observe destructive behaviors that subvert the team's performance within the workplace, do you intervene or look the other way?
2. Do you understand the corrosive effects these problems can have both on a team and an organization?

TRAINING ACTIVITY – APPLICATION & ACTION PLAN

1. Listed below are the five subversive team roles:
    - Cutting or Shutting Off Discussion
    - Analyzing and Labeling
    - Dominating
    - 'Yes Butting'
    - Nay Saying
2. Identify specific statements that can be used to neutralize and reverse each of the destructive behaviors listed above.

6

Building Strength and Energizing the Team

The essence of leadership is found in team building and development where leaders apply specific skills to the task of bringing a diverse group of individuals together into an effective working team.

IMPLICATIONS – WHAT THIS MEANS TO YOU

Leadership is ultimately an act of faith in other people. Adhering to their personal vision, leaders apply specific skills and abilities to energizing, motivating and guiding the action and direction of their teams. Additionally, leaders use their ability to delegate authority and empower their teams to implement and execute the specific strategies developed within the team environment. However, it is a mistake for leaders to assume that teams can totally operate on their own without guidance, direction and intervention from their leaders.

Within the team environment, leaders need to exert specific skills that allow them to share their vision and develop cooperation that ultimately creates a synergy that energizes the team and makes it thrive. Without active leadership, many working groups and teams will ultimately become lost and ineffective. It is important for leaders not only to cheer and motivate their teams, but also to guide and direct them.

STRATEGIES, TIPS & TECHNIQUES TO APPLY

Leaders must understand that they cannot simply label a group of individuals as a team or working group and then expect them to automatically blend themselves into an effective working unit. Rather, leaders must be actively involved and exert direct leadership upon their teams in order for them to develop and build the strength that energizes their actions and direction. The elements that build team strength and energy include:

Shared Vision

One of the hallmarks of effective leadership is a personal vision defining where it is leaders think the organization should be heading. One of the first tasks leaders should focus on when developing effective work teams is that of communicating their personal vision to their team. However, communication alone is not sufficient; leaders must also sell their teams on the vision so that it becomes a shared driving force for the entire team.

Mutual Goals

When teams and working groups are ultimately established, individual team members bring a diverse group of goals and objectives to the table. Leaders must blend those goals and objectives so that all team members share those that best fit the interests of the team. As this occurs, individual team members will set aside their personal goals and agendas for those of the team.

Shared Purpose

People are naturally driven to work toward something larger than themselves. As teams develop and blend, they create a shared purpose that motivates and energizes individual team members toward the accomplishment of collective goals and objectives. These individual members understand that accomplishment of a shared purpose is greater than what they can achieve on their own.

Mutual Respect

One of the hallmarks of effective teams is the mutual respect that individual team members have for one another regardless of their divergent viewpoints and perspectives. When destructive personal behaviors that sap team strength are eliminated and people understand the value of the feedback and contributions made by all team members, mutual respect is developed and cultivated. A critical aspect of the team culture, this respect is nurtured by team rules, roles and boundaries. Any undermining of mutual respect within the team is corrosive and destructive to the future actions of the team.

Imbedded Best Practices

As organizations change and evolve and teams are developed and dismantled, specific best practices that have evolved and been proven over time should become crystallized and imbedded within the organization. These best practices eliminate the need for each and every team to "reinvent the wheel" and allow them to get a jump start on their programs and projects. However, over time some "best practices" can become outmoded and outdated, used only because of their duration and implementation by other teams. Leaders should observe and review their best practices to assure that they are both effective and productive and do not hinder the performance of their teams.

Time to Develop and Grow

Team development must be fostered by allowing teams the time to go through various stages of development and grow into effective working units. As each team is unique, development time will vary according to the experience and expertise of its members. Experienced and seasoned individuals who have worked together previously can appreciably shorten the time required to build team strength and develop into a working unit.

Setting Their Own Direction

Teams build strength, energize and motivate themselves when they are given the space to set their own direction. While leaders play an active role in guiding and directing their team, they should allow it the latitude to create its own rules, roles, boundaries, goals and ultimate direction.

Within some organizational settings, effective teams can become self-managing with minimal intervention by leaders; in other environments, active leadership intervention, direction and guidance is required. The degree of guidance and direction will depend on the maturity and responsibilities of individual team members. The overall goal of leaders should be to incrementally surrender more of their authority to their teams. As teams grow and demonstrate their effectiveness, leaders will develop increased confidence in their ability to assume specific roles, authority and responsibility.

POINTS TO PONDER — SOMETHING TO THINK ABOUT

1. How actively do you exert your leadership within the team environment?
2. What have you observed when leaders have failed to take an active role in their team's development?

TRAINING ACTIVITY — APPLICATION & ACTION PLAN

1. Listed below are the specific elements that build team strength, energize and motivate teams.
    - Shared Vision
    - Mutual Goals
    - Shared Purpose
    - Mutual Respect
    - Imbedded Best Practices
    - Time to Develop and Grow
    - Setting Their Own Direction

2. For each of these building strategies, create and identify specific examples that you have observed within your organization.
3. Review and analyze each specific example.
4. Identify the specific lessons learned from each example.
5. Determine how best to apply the lessons learned to your entire team environment.

7

Auditing for Monitoring Overall Team Strength

Leaders cannot assume that teams will automatically police and monitor themselves. Rather, leaders need to regularly audit a team's performance to ensure that the mechanisms that build overall strength are firmly in place.

IMPLICATIONS – WHAT THIS MEANS TO YOU

The fact that leaders are dealing with human nature makes team behaviors unpredictable and impacted by a number of variables that may or may not be within their control.

A single individual has the ability to undermine and ultimately destroy team strength. Consequently, leaders must continually audit the team's overall performance. Such an audit requires both time and attention to detail when observing the behaviors, attitudes and levels of participation reflected within the team.

STRATEGIES, TIPS & TECHNIQUES TO APPLY

Leaders should audit the following areas on an ongoing basis in order to maintain overall team strength.

Participation

Leaders must ensure both balanced and equal levels of participation exist throughout the team. They must ensure that all individual members participate in the team process and are given equal opportunities to offer their insights and feedback. In this regard, leaders must make sure that no individual team member dominates the environment or is allowed to cow any other participants into silence.

Interaction

Leaders must actively observe the levels of interaction between individual team members. An active team will have open and energetic levels of communication, where members are openly and freely working with one another. Leaders must be aware of whether specific team members seem to be left out of the process, and identify those who may be reluctant to participate, have been intimidated into silence or had their behaviors minimized by more demanding and dominant members of the team.

Level of Development

Leaders must actively monitor the team's overall level of development and maturity. A healthy team will grow, mature and become seasoned in their actions and decisions. While such development might occur in incremental steps that are difficult to monitor, leaders should take the time to evaluate the progress and growth of the team over prolonged periods of time.

Mutual Levels of Respect

Leaders should be observant for the mutual levels of respect demonstrated by team members. As teams develop, mature, and become more seasoned, the overall respect demonstrated by individual team members should be increasing and readily evident. Leaders must audit for both minimizing and destructive behaviors that reflect a lack of respect and undermine the entire team's performance.

Depth and Scope

Leaders should also be auditing their team for the depth and scope of their brainstorming and decision making. Initially, teams will be dealing superficially with their projects or topics. As they mature and grow within the process, the breadth and scope of their brainstorming, analysis and decision making should increase and reflect the maturity of the team. If leaders conclude that these levels have not increased, they must take the appropriate action to challenge their team to grow.

Synergy

A sure sign that a team has developed and evolved is the synergy reflected in its actions and decisions. As team members learn to work with one another toward mutual goals and objectives, the overall synergy of the group should expand to the point where the whole becomes greater that the sum of the parts. Leaders who have determined that sufficient cooperation has not been developed should review the five aforementioned areas, as each will impact the overall level of synergy.

POINTS TO PONDER – SOMETHING TO THINK ABOUT

1. How closely do you audit and monitor the behaviors, attitudes and activities within your team environment?
2. Do you observe a healthy level of synergy as your team develops strength and maturity?

TRAINING ACTIVITY – APPLICATION & ACTION PLAN

1. Cite specific examples in each of the following categories, positive or negative, within your team environment:

- Participation
- Interaction
- Level of Development
- Mutual Levels of Respect
- Depth and Scope
- Synergy

2. Identify specific signs that indicate both a healthy and an unhealthy team environment.
3. Determine the specific actions needed when negative signs and unhealthy behavior are identified.

8

Sustaining Team Growth

Some leaders might consider team development and growth a panacea leading to a perfect decision making environment. However, as leaders must deal with individuals and a mix of personalities, attitudes and motivations, this is often far from the case. While this is the reality most leaders must confront in the team environment, many of these human tendencies can be overcome and corrected with time.

IMPLICATIONS – WHAT THIS MEANS TO YOU

Leaders tend to expect greater productivity and effectiveness as teams mature and develop. However, since they are dealing with the human factor—including immature and unresponsive team members—they soon discover that certain individuals can undermine and sabotage the team and its mission. It should be noted that dominant team members, as well as overbearing leaders, can create the same environment.

It is important for leaders to understand that teams must be balanced in their behavior, motivation and attitude. As they mature and learn to work together, the results they produce will positively impact their behavior. Leaders must learn not only to balance their own behaviors, but also those of all individual team members.

STRATEGIES, TIPS & TECHNIQUES TO APPLY

When their team is properly managed, leaders should have specific expectations that it will ultimately fulfill. These include:

Evolution

All teams will go through a natural evolutionary process as participants learn to work with and respect one another. As teams grow and develop, they should learn how to monitor their members and eliminate both negative and destructive behaviors from the environment.

Maturity

As teams achieve specific levels of development, the team also matures in their actions, decisions and behaviors. This is part of the natural evolutionary process that allows teams to become more effective and productive over prolonged periods of time.

However, leaders should understand that some teams will never mature. This is reflected by the presence of "Dilbert" cartoons in many corporate cubicles. Undoubtedly, the lack of maturity reflected by both leaders and individual team members can cause an overall stagnation and lack of productivity within the team environment. This is one reason why leaders must learn to effectively audit the team process.

Self-Direction

As teams mature, develop and evolve, they can ultimately reach the point of becoming wholly self-directed. This occurs when all individual team members understand the rules, goals, boundaries and duties required of them. They learn to work together and assume all these roles in a responsible manner.

Productivity

An increase in overall productivity is the ultimate goal toward which leaders want to direct their teams. Progress is made when individual teams learn to effectively tackle new projects and assignments on their own. They automatically know how and when to proceed without the direction of management and leadership. They undertake their assignments responsibly and perform them in an efficient and timely manner.

Motivation

The results produced by the team collectively are greater than the contribution of each member. As these results breed further successes, the team should be motivated to tackle larger and more challenging tasks and assignments. However, leaders should recognize that in any environment there will always be individuals who will remain unmotivated and unresponsive. As teams develop and evolve, they should be capable of monitoring these members' behaviors. In some cases leaders may need to counsel and mentor certain individuals directly, and if they do not respond, ultimately remove these people from the team environment.

POINTS TO PONDER – SOMETHING TO THINK ABOUT

1. What are your expectations of your working teams?
2. Are effective teams seriously considered within your corporate environment?

TRAINING ACTIVITY – APPLICATION & ACTION PLAN

1. Think of the specific expectations you have of your team.
2. Identify the specific team reality that you have observed in your work place.
3. Determine the key differences between your expectations and reality and the specific reasons why they exist.
4. Decide what you can do to make that reality match your expectations.

About the Author

Timothy F. Bednarz, Ph.D. is CEO of the American Management Development Group, Inc. For over 20 years he has researched, designed and authored hundreds of learning and development programs used by Fortune 1000 companies.

He is also the author of *Great! What Makes Leaders Great. What They Did, How They Did It and What You Can Learn from It* (2011).

Speaking Availability

Timothy F. Bednarz, Ph.D. is available for speaking engagements for your next meeting or association event. He can be contacted at 800-654-4935 or by e-mail at timothy.bednarz@majorium.com.

Bulk Sales

Bulk sales of this book or any other titles available from Majorium Business Press. Inquiries can be directed to sales@majorium.com, or by phone at 800-6654-4935.

Quick Order Form

Fax orders: 715-342-1118. Send this form.

Telephone orders: Call 800-654-4935 toll-free. Have your credit card ready.

Email orders: sales@majorium.com

Postal orders: Majorium Business Press, 2025 Main Street, Stevens Point, WI 54481, USA.

Please send the following books:

____

____

____

____

Please send more FREE information on:

❑Catalog ❑Speaking/Seminars ❑Mailing Lists ❑Consulting

Name: ____________________________________

Address: __________________________________

City: ____________________ State: _____ Zip: __________

Telephone: ________________________________

Email address: ______________________________

Sales tax: Please add 5.5% for products shipped to Wisconsin addresses.

Shipping by air:

United States: $4.00 for first book and $2.00 for each additional product.

International: $9.00 for first book; $5.00 for each additional product (estimate).

Made in United States
Cleveland, OH
05 November 2026

47664310R00030